New Testament Tales

from The Lion Storyteller Bible

Retold by Bob Hartman

Illustrations by Susie Poole

LION
Children's Books

Text copyright © 1995 Bob Hartman
Illustrations copyright © 1995 Susie Poole
This edition copyright © 2000 Lion Publishing

The moral rights of the author and illustrator
have been asserted

Published by
Lion Publishing plc
Sandy Lane West, Oxford, England
www.lion-publishing.co.uk
ISBN 0 7459 4405 1

First edition 2000
10 9 8 7 6 5 4 3 2 1 0

A catalogue record for this book is available
from the British Library

Printed and bound in Spain

Contents

The First Christmas

'Good news!' said the angel to a girl named Mary. 'God is sending Someone Special into the world. He will be a great king. His name will be Jesus. And guess what? God wants you to be his mother!'

'Good news!' said the angel to a carpenter named Joseph. 'God is sending Someone Special into the world. He will rescue everyone from the wrong things they have done. He will be God's own Son! But guess what? God wants you to take his mother Mary as your wife, and raise little Jesus as your own.'

'Bad news!' sighed Joseph to Mary. 'The rulers of our country want to count us, to see how many of us there are. And to make it easier for them, we have to go back to our home town. That means a trip all the way from Nazareth to Bethlehem! And with the baby due so soon...'

'Bad news!' sighed the innkeeper, shaking his head. 'There's not one room left in Bethlehem. But seeing as the young lady's expecting and all, why don't you spend the night in my stable?'

'Good news!' smiled Joseph, handing the baby to Mary. 'It's a boy, just as God promised. God's own Son, there in your arms—Jesus.'

'Good news!' called the angel to the shepherds on the hill. 'God has sent Someone Special into the world. The someone you have been waiting for. If you hurry into Bethlehem, you can see him for yourselves. He's just a baby now, wrapped up warmly and lying in a manger. But one day he will save you from all that is wrong. One day he will bring you peace!'

Then the angels filled the sky with a good news song. The shepherds went to Bethlehem and made a good news visit. And, on that very first Christmas Day, Mary just watched, and rocked her baby, and smiled a good news smile!

The Wise Men's Visit

The sky was black. The night was clear. The stars were bright as diamonds.

'Perfect,' said the star-watcher. 'Just as it should be.' But just then God nudged the brightest star and sent it floating like a kite across the night sky.

'Quick,' called the star-watcher to his friends. 'Come and see. There's a new star and that means...'

'... a new king!' said the second star-watcher. 'Somewhere a new king is about to be born!'

'I'll tell you what,' said the third star-watcher, 'let's follow the star and see.'

So the three star-watchers climbed onto their camels and set off after the star. When it zigged, they zigged. When it zagged, they zagged—across deserts and mountains and rivers. Until they reached the land of God's people, the Jews.

'We have come a long way,' explained the first star-watcher to King Herod.

'We have followed a remarkable star,' explained the second star-watcher.

'So can you tell us where the baby is?' asked the third star-watcher. 'The baby born King of the Jews?'

'King of the Jews? King of the Jews?' King Herod repeated, trying hard not to look upset. 'Let me speak with my advisers.'

And so King Herod called a meeting. A meeting that was not very happy.

'King of the Jews?' the king shouted. 'King of the Jews? I AM THE KING OF THE JEWS!!'

'Y-yes, Your Majesty,' his advisers mumbled. 'But God has always promised that one day he would send us a special king. P-perhaps he is the one the star-watchers are looking for.'

'Hmm,' Herod muttered. 'And where does God say this special king will be born?'

'In Bethlehem, Your Majesty. The city of David.'

'Send for the star-watchers,' King Herod ordered. 'I have decided what I shall do.'

'Gentlemen,' said the king, 'the child you seek is somewhere in Bethlehem. Go to him. Find him. Then come and tell me where he is, so that I can visit him, too.'

The king said this with a smile, but his heart was black, black as a night without stars. And he had already determined to kill the child, so no one would take his place as king.

The star-watchers didn't know that when they left, but they soon found out. For the same God who had nudged the star visited them in a dream and told them the king's dark plan.

So they went to see young Jesus, and gave him gifts of gold and frankincense and myrrh. And then they went straight home, with stars in their eyes and God in their hearts.

Jesus' Special Friends

Jesus grew up in a place called Galilee, where there was a large and beautiful lake. And it was there that he began the work God gave him to do.

'God is like a king,' he told the people. 'And he wants all of you to be a part of his kingdom—to love him and to love each other.'

People liked to hear Jesus talk. In fact, one morning, the crowd was so huge that Jesus was nearly pushed into the sea.

'Excuse me,' Jesus asked a fisherman, 'could I borrow your boat for a while?'

The fisherman's name was Peter. 'Of course,' he said. 'It's doing me no good. I was out all night and didn't catch a thing.'

Jesus climbed into the boat. Peter rowed it a little way from shore. And, from there, Jesus talked to the crowd. When he had finished, Jesus sent the people home. And then he turned to Peter.

'Let's go a little further out,' he whispered. 'I'd like to catch some fish.'

Peter tossed back his head and laughed. 'I told you. Me and my men were out all night. We caught nothing!'

Jesus didn't say a word. He just smiled and looked across the lake.

'All right,' Peter sighed. 'If that's what you want.'

So Peter sailed to the deepest part of the lake. Then he dropped his fishing nets over the side.

It took no time at all. The nets started pulling and jerking and stretching. And it was all Peter could do to keep the boat from tipping over.

'Help!' Peter called to some friends nearby. 'Help me, please!' And they rowed to him as fast as they could.

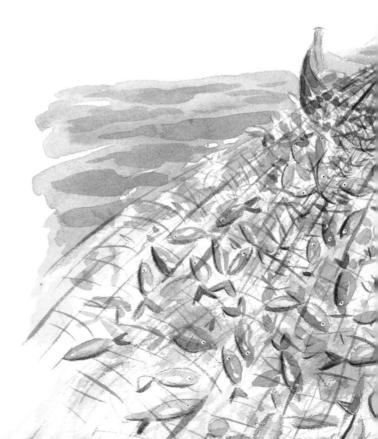

Then, all together, the men pulled on the nets—and the fish came tumbling and slapping onto the decks of both boats. Red fish and blue fish, not just one or two fish. So many, in fact, that the boats would have sunk, had the fishermen not rowed quickly back to shore.

Peter looked at the fish. Peter looked at his friends. Then Peter looked at Jesus, and fell to his knees, trembling.

'Only God, or somebody full of his power, could do that,' Peter said. 'And why would someone like that want to go fishing with the likes of me?'

Jesus shook his head and smiled. 'Don't be scared,' he said. 'God has given me a lot of work to do. And I need helpers. Helpers like you and your friends. Once you were fishermen. But from now on, you'll be fishing for people. And helping me bring them to God.'

Then Jesus stepped out of the boat and walked away, across the shore. 'Come with me,' he called.

Peter and his friends watched him go. They looked at the fish. They looked at each other. Then they dropped their nets, left their boats behind, and raced off to follow Jesus.

The Storm on the Lake

It was a perfect day.

The sky was blue. The lake, too.

And a gentle breeze whipped the wave tips white and foamy.

Jesus sat at the side of the lake and talked to the people about God.

'God is your Father,' he said. 'He dresses the flowers in beautiful colours. He makes sure the birds have enough to eat. But you are his sons and his daughters. Don't you think he can clothe and feed you, too? So trust him, and stop worrying your lives away.'

When Jesus had finished teaching, he was tired. So he called his closest friends, and together they piled into a boat and set off across the lake for home.

Jesus yawned. He stretched. He laid his head down and, to the rhythm of the waves and the rocking of the boat, he fell asleep. It was the perfect end to a perfect day!

And then, suddenly, the day was not so perfect.

The sky turned black. The lake, too.

And a wild wind stirred the waves up tall and stormy.

The boat rocked right. The boat rocked left. The boat rocked up and down. The boat rocked so hard, in fact, that Jesus' friends were sure they would all drown.

But Jesus slept right through it—except for the odd snuffle and snore.

'Jesus!' his friends called at last. 'Jesus! Wake up! We're all going to drown!'

So Jesus woke up. Then he sat up. Then he rubbed his eyes and he stood up. It was all anybody else could do to stay on their feet. But Jesus stood up! And then, very calmly, he said to the wind, 'Quiet now.' And he said to the waves, 'Settle down.'

And they did!

Then Jesus turned to his friends and said, 'You didn't need to be frightened. You didn't have to worry. All you had to do was trust me. See, everything is calm.'

And so it was. The sky was blue. The lake, too. And the little waves splashed happily at the side of the boat.

It was a perfect day, again!

'Time to Get Up'

'Jesus! Help me, Jesus! My daughter is dying!' Jairus shouted as loud as he could, and the crowd parted to let him through.

'She's only twelve,' he explained. 'And she's so ill. But I know I can count on you to make her well. Please!'

Jesus nodded. 'Show me the way,' he said. But the minute they started wading through the crowd, Jesus stopped.

'Somebody touched me,' he whispered.

'Jesus,' one of his friends whispered back, 'there are hundreds of people here. I'm sure lots of them touched you.'

'No,' said Jesus, raising his voice now. 'Somebody here was sick. Very sick. Then they touched me and God made them well. I felt it. I felt the power rush out of me! Now, who was it?'

'It was me,' said a woman close by. 'I have been sick for so long. I've spent so much money on doctors. But when I touched your robe, I was healed!'

Jesus turned to the woman and smiled. He was so happy for her. 'You trusted me,' he said. 'That's good. So God has made you well.'

'Jesus,' said Jairus. 'Jesus, I don't mean to interrupt...'

But before Jairus could say another word, one of his servants called out across the crowd, 'Master, master, I have the most awful news...'

Jairus knew it even before the servant spoke.

'... your daughter is dead.'

Jesus turned from the happy woman to the sad father.

'It will be all right,' he said. 'Trust me.' Then they hurried off to Jairus' house.

When they arrived, there was another crowd—wailing and weeping in front of the house. The sad news had spread fast.

'Listen, everybody,' said Jesus. 'There's no need to cry. The girl is not dead. She's only sleeping.'

Sad tears gave way to angry laughter. 'Don't be ridiculous!' someone shouted. 'We've seen her. She's dead!'

Jesus ignored them all. He asked the girl's mother and father, and three of his friends, Peter, James and John, to come with him. Together they walked straight to where the girl was lying.

She certainly looked dead. Her eyes were closed. Her face was pale. Her skin was cold. But that didn't stop Jesus. He took her cold hand in his and called, 'Little girl, little girl, it's time to get up.'

Her skin grew warm. Her face flushed pink. And her eyelids flickered and flew open. She was alive!

And the first thing she said was, 'I'm hungry!'

'Then we'd better get you something to eat,' said Jesus.

And it was the best meal that family ever had.

The Marvellous Picnic

It wasn't long before lots of people wanted to hear Jesus talk about God. And many more wanted him to make them well. So they followed him everywhere. From town to town. From city to country. And all the way back again.

'We need a rest,' Jesus said to his friends, one day. So they took a little boat trip across Lake Galilee, hoping to camp for a while in the hills beyond. But the people were so eager to see Jesus that they raced around the shoreline to meet him on the other side!

Jesus was tired. But when he turned and saw the people following him up the hill, he stopped. 'They're like sheep without a shepherd,' he said to his friends. 'They need someone to show them the way.'

So he sat himself down—right then and there. And he started to teach.

'God loves you,' Jesus said. 'He knows what's best for you. The most amazing things can happen when you trust him.'

Jesus said a lot more than that. He taught all day, in fact. And, by then, the people were hungry.

'Philip!' Jesus called to one of his friends. 'Can you go out and buy some food for these people?'

Philip just laughed. 'There are more than five thousand of them! It would take six months' pay to feed them all.'

Then Andrew, Peter's brother, spoke up. 'There's a boy here, Jesus, who has a little food. Five loaves of bread and a couple of fish. It's not much, but it's a start.'

'So it is,' grinned Jesus, and he rubbed his hands together, as if he were about to go to work. 'Make the people sit down in little groups. Tell them we're going to have a picnic!'

Jesus' friends looked at Jesus. They looked at the boy's little lunch. They looked at the enormous crowd. Then they looked at each other and shrugged.

'All right,' they agreed. 'Whatever you say.'

Jesus smiled as he watched them go. Then he bowed his head, thanked God for the food, and started breaking it into pieces. The friends returned and began to pass out the pieces. And, to their amazement, there was plenty for the first group, and the second group, and the third group, and then every group! Plenty for everyone. More than enough to go around. So much, in fact, that there were twelve baskets full of leftovers to take home!

The people patted their tummies. They struggled to their feet. They wiped the crumbs from their mouths. And some even burped!

But all Jesus' friends could do was stare.

'It's just as I told you,' said Jesus. 'God can do the most amazing things. All we have to do is trust him.'

Then he smiled at his helpers, popped a chunk of bread into his mouth, and started off for home.

The Kind Stranger

Jesus was teaching one day when a man in the crowd asked him a question.

'Can you tell me, Jesus, what I have to do to live for ever?'

Jesus smiled. 'Love God,' he answered, 'and love your neighbour as much as you love yourself.'

'But who is my neighbour?' asked the man, hoping to trick Jesus. 'Is he just the fellow who lives next door?'

'Let me tell you a story,' Jesus said, 'and I think you will understand.'

'Once upon a time, there was a man—a man like any one of us—who was travelling from Jerusalem to Jericho. Now as you all know, that is a very dangerous road. It's twisty and it's steep, and there's no end of places for robbers and thieves to hide.

'Well, the robbers were waiting that day. And they grabbed the man. And they beat him. And they took his money and left him to die.'

'Oh dear,' sighed the crowd. They felt sorry for the man.

Jesus went on with his story.

'In a little while, another man came walking down that road—a priest, on his way home from worshipping God at the temple. He saw the dying man, and what do you think he did?'

'He helped him!' shouted someone in the crowd.

'He saved him!' shouted another.

'No!' said Jesus, firmly. 'He did not. He took one look at that poor, beaten man, crossed to the other side of the road, and walked away.'

'Oh my,' the crowd murmured.

'Wait,' Jesus continued. 'Soon another man passed by. He served God at the temple, too. So what do you think this man did when he saw the wounded traveller?'

'He ran for help!' shouted someone.

'He raised the alarm!' shouted another.

'No!' said Jesus, again. 'He did not. Just like the priest, he crossed to the other side of the road and left that poor man to die.'

'Oh no,' the crowd sighed.

'Don't worry,' said Jesus. 'For there was one more man who passed by that day. And he was a Samaritan.'

'A Samaritan?' shouted someone. 'They're different from us!'

'We hate Samaritans!' shouted another.

'And they hate us!' added a third.

'So I've heard,' nodded Jesus. 'But when

this Samaritan saw the man, he did not walk away. No. He bandaged his wounds. He loaded him on his donkey. He took him to a nearby inn. And he paid for that man to stay there until he was well.'

Jesus looked at the man who had asked him the question. 'So tell me,' he said, 'which of these men was a neighbour to the man who had been robbed?'

'The third one. The Samaritan,' the man answered.

'That's right,' Jesus smiled. 'Because my neighbour is anyone who needs my help. Now you go and help your neighbour, too.'

The Big Spender

The people who thought they were good were still not happy with Jesus. They moaned. They grumbled. They frowned.

'It's not fair,' they complained. 'Jesus spends all his time with the bad people.'

Jesus heard this and told them one more story:

'Once upon a time there was a man who had two sons. He loved them both, very much. But one day, the younger son came to him with a sad request.

"Father," the younger son said, "when you die, I will get part of your money and part of your land. The problem is, I don't want to wait. I want my money now!"

It was all the father could do to hold back his tears. But because he loved his son, he agreed, and gave him his share of the money.

That very day the son left home, money in his pocket and a big smile on his face. He didn't even say goodbye. The father just watched, wiped away a tear, and hoped that one day he would see his son again.

The son travelled to a country far, far away and spent his money just as fast as he could. He drank. He gambled. He used his money to do many bad things—until finally the money was gone.

The son looked for a job, but the only work he could find was taking care of pigs! It was hard, dirty work, and he was so hungry sometimes that he thought about taking the pigs' food for himself. He was miserable, lonely, and sad. And then one day, he had an idea.

18

"The servants who take care of my father's animals are much happier than me. I'll go home, that's what I'll do. I'll tell my father how sorry I am for wasting his money. And maybe, just maybe, he'll let me become a servant and work for him."

Now what do you think the father had been doing all this time? Did he say to himself, "I have my eldest son at home with me. Who cares if my younger son is gone?" Of course not! He loved his son, even though he had gone far away. And every day, he would go out to the roadside and watch, hoping his son would return.

That's exactly where he was when the younger son hobbled home, poor and hungry. The father ran to his son and hugged him tight. And the son dropped right to his knees.

"Oh, Father," he cried. "I'm so sorry. I have wasted all your money and am no longer good enough to be your son."

"Don't be silly," said the father. "You are my son. You will always be my son. And I am so glad to have you back!" Then the father lifted his son to his feet and walked him home. He dressed him in beautiful clothes. He put gold rings on his fingers. And he threw him a big welcome home party.

When the elder son came home from work that night, he heard the party noise.

"What's happening?" he asked. And when a servant told him, he was filled with anger and ran to his father.

"It's not fair!" he shouted. "I've been a good son. I've worked hard for you all these years. But he was bad. He wasted your money. And now you're throwing him a party."

"I love you, my son," the father said. "And you have enjoyed all the good things I have. But your brother was gone, and now he's back. He was lost, and now he's found. That's why I'm having this party, because we're all back together again." '

The Man Who Came Back

One, two, three,
  Four, five, six,
  Seven, eight, nine,
  And ten.
  There were ten lepers on the road, one day. And no one would go near them. Their fingers were numb. Their faces were scarred. They were terribly, terribly ill.
  One, two, three,
  Four, five, six,
  Seven, eight, nine,
  And ten.
  There were ten lepers on the road, one day. And Jesus came walking by. 'Jesus!' they cried. 'Oh, Jesus!' they begged. 'Save us. Please make us well!'

One, two, three,
  Four, five, six,
  Seven, eight, nine,
  And ten.
  There were ten lepers on the road, one day. And Jesus prayed for them. 'Now go!' he said. 'Go. Find a priest, and he'll tell you if you are well.'
  One, two, three,
  Four, five, six,
  Seven, eight, nine,
  And ten.
  There were ten lepers on the road, that day. And then suddenly there weren't! Their fingers were fine. Their faces like new! They were happy and healed and whole!

One, two, three,
Four, five, six,
Seven, eight,
And nine.
Nine lepers (who weren't lepers any more!) rushed off to share their good news. But leper number ten went straight back to Jesus, to thank him for what he had done.

One, two, three,
Four, five, six,
Seven, eight, nine,
And ten.
'I healed ten lepers on the road today,' said Jesus to the man. 'But where are the rest? Never mind, I'm just pleased that you came back to thank me!'

Jesus and the Children

'I can't see!' called a blind woman. 'Can you help me, Jesus?'

'I can't walk!' called a lame man. 'Heal me, Jesus, please!'

'He can't hear!' called a deaf man's friend. 'Touch him, Jesus, and make him well.'

They were everywhere—people with every kind of sickness. And Jesus felt sorry for them all. So he did what he could to help the crowd that day.

'I can't see,' said a little girl to her mother. 'There are too many people in the way.'

'I can't move,' said her little brother. 'We're all squashed in here.'

'What did you say?' asked their father. 'I can't hear. This crowd is so noisy!'

'Excuse me,' said their mother to one of Jesus' friends. 'We were wondering if Jesus could pray for our children.'

'Are they sick?' asked the friend.

'No,' the mother answered. 'We just wanted Jesus to ask God to watch over them and protect them.'

'I see,' said the friend impatiently. 'Well, as you have noticed, Jesus is a very busy man. He has important things to do. Lots of sick people to make well.'

'That's right!' added another of Jesus' friends. 'There are grown-ups here who need his help. He can't be bothered with children.'

'Particularly children who aren't even sick!' chimed in a third friend. 'It's just a waste of his time.'

The mother and the father and the children looked at each other. Then they looked at the ground and turned to leave. They were sad and embarrassed.

'Does this mean we won't see Jesus?' asked the little girl, rubbing the tears from her eyes.

But before her mother could answer, another voice called out across the crowd. 'Wait!' It was the voice of Jesus!

'Bring your children here,' Jesus called. 'There's nothing to be ashamed of.' And he gave his friends an unhappy look.

Jesus picked up the little boy and the little girl and set them on his lap. He gave them each a hug, and then he said, 'Listen. I want everybody to listen. Particularly my friends. You must never keep the children away from me. They are as important to me as anyone else. And I want to be their friend, too.

'Don't you see? God wants us all to be like these children. To love him like a father. To trust him completely. And to long to be with him.'

Then Jesus prayed for the children, hugged them one more time, and sent them beaming back to their parents.

Jesus and the Taxman

'Jesus is coming!' somebody shouted. 'Jesus is coming to Jericho!' And everybody ran to meet him.

Well, almost everybody. For there was one man—one wee little man—who did not run to meet Jesus. And his name was Zacchaeus.

It's not that Zacchaeus didn't want to see Jesus. He did. He really did. But, not only was Zacchaeus short, he was also afraid of the crowd. Not many people liked him, you see. Partly because he was a tax collector. But mostly because he collected more taxes than he was supposed to—and kept what was left for himself.

'Jesus is here!' somebody shouted. 'Jesus is here in Jericho!' And everybody cheered as he walked through the city gates.

Well, almost everybody. For Zacchaeus did not feel like cheering at all. He wanted to see Jesus. He really did. But how could he walk out there in front of all those people he'd cheated? And what would they do if they got hold of him?

Then Zacchaeus had an idea. There were trees by the city gates—tall, leafy trees. If he could sneak behind the crowd and climb one of those trees, he could see Jesus—and not be seen himself!

So off he went—out of his house and through the empty streets. And because the crowd was watching Jesus, he had no trouble at all slipping behind them and shinning up a tree.

'Come, eat at my house!' somebody shouted. 'Come, eat at my house, Jesus!' And because it was a great honour to host someone as important as Jesus, everybody shouted at once.

Well, almost everybody. For there was one man—one wee little man—who kept his mouth shut and tried hard not to rustle the branches.

'Thank you very much,' said Jesus. 'You are very kind. But I have already decided where I will eat my dinner.'

Then Jesus looked straight at the trees and called, 'Zacchaeus! Zacchaeus, come down! I'm eating at your house today.'

'Zacchaeus?' somebody shouted. 'Jesus is eating with Zacchaeus? He's the worst man in town. There must be some mistake!' And everybody moaned and groaned.

Well, almost everybody. One man—one wee little man—climbed down from the tree, as shocked as the rest. Why would someone as good as Jesus want to eat with someone bad like him? But he was happy, too. Happier than he'd been for a long, long time. And so, with a smile spreading across his face, Zacchaeus led Jesus to his house.

'What are they saying?' somebody whispered. 'What are they doing in there?' And everybody gathered around the taxman's door.

That's when Zacchaeus threw open his door with a bang!

'Greetings, everyone!' he shouted. 'I have an announcement to make. I've been talking with my new friend, Jesus, and realize that there are a few things I need to change. I've cheated some of you. I admit that. And I want you to know that I'm sorry. So sorry, in fact, that I will pay you back four times more than I stole from you! What's more, I intend to sell half of what I own and give the money to the poor!'

The crowd was shocked. Never, in their whole lives, had they seen anyone change like that! They stood there with their mouths wide open. And nobody said a thing.

Well, almost nobody.

'Don't you see?' said Jesus to the crowd. 'God has sent me to share his love with everybody—even those who have done some very bad things. That's what I have done. And now Zacchaeus loves God, too.'

That's when the crowd began to cheer. Jesus. And Zacchaeus. And the whole town of Jericho.

Everybody.

An Important Meal

Jesus and his twelve friends sat down to eat. There was lamb and bread and wine. A nice meal. But Jesus was sad.

'What's the matter, Jesus?' asked one of his friends.

'I have to go away tomorrow,' Jesus sighed. 'And I will miss you very much.'

Jesus' friends were surprised. 'Where are you going?' they asked.

'I am going to be with my Father in heaven,' he whispered. 'I am going to die.'

Now Jesus' friends were sad, too.

'There are people here in Jerusalem who do not like me,' Jesus explained. 'They do not agree with what I teach. They do not believe I come from God. And tomorrow they will arrest me and hurt me and nail me to a cross and kill me.'

'No!' said Jesus' friends. 'They will not do that. We will not let them!'

Jesus looked at them sadly. 'One of you has already taken money from them and agreed to help them catch me.'

Jesus' friends stared at each other.

'Well, it's not me!' said one.

'It's not me,' said another.

But one of them—a man named Judas— just looked at Jesus, then stood up and walked out of the room.

'Let him go,' Jesus told the others. 'We have something more important to do.'

And with that, Jesus took a chunk of bread and said a thank-you prayer.

'I will never forget you,' he said to his friends. 'And I don't want you to forget me either.' Then he broke the bread in half and passed it round. 'This is my body,' he said. 'I give it up for you. Take it and eat it and remember me.'

Then he took a cup of wine and said a thank-you prayer for that, as well.

'This is my blood,' he said. 'God will use it to wash away all the bad things anyone has ever done. Take it and drink it and remember me.'

Then Jesus and his friends sang a goodbye song and walked out together into the night.

A Dreadful Day

When Jesus and his friends had finished their goodbye meal, they walked to a garden to pray. That's where Jesus' enemies found him.

The men had torches and clubs and sticks. They were very frightening. And right in front was Judas, who had been one of Jesus' friends.

Judas crept up to Jesus and kissed him on the cheek. 'This is the man you want!' said Judas. 'Arrest him!' Jesus looked very sad.

Jesus' friends were scared. Most of them ran away. But not Peter. He pulled out a sword and started swinging it about.

'Put your sword away,' said Jesus. 'This is not the time for fighting. I have to go with them. God wants me to.'

So they grabbed Jesus, and dragged him before the religious leaders—the ones who were jealous of him. His trial took all night.

'He says he will destroy our temple,' said one man.

'He says he is a king,' said another.

'He's a troublemaker!' said one and all.

None of this was true, of course. But it didn't matter, because the leaders had already made up their minds. Jesus was different from them. Jesus wouldn't do what they said. So Jesus would have to die.

They beat Jesus. They hit him hard. Then they took away his clothes, put an old robe round his shoulders, and jammed a crown made of thorns on his head. And while the blood ran down his forehead, they called him names and made fun of him. 'So you think you're a king?' they laughed. 'Well, look at you now!'

Jesus never said a word. His body hurt, his heart was breaking, but he never said a word.

They took a cross, next, made of heavy wood, and they laid it on his back. 'Move along!' they shouted, and they led him through the city. Some people cried when they saw him. Others cheered. But all of them followed, as he lugged that cross through the city gates and up a nearby hill.

When they got to the top, they laid Jesus on the cross and nailed him to it. It hurt so much. Then they raised the cross, so that everyone could see, and they left him there to die.

A thief, hanging next to him, was afraid. But Jesus talked to him and helped him feel better.

Jesus' mother was there, too, standing in

the crowd. So Jesus called to one of his friends, 'Take care of her for me, will you, John? She's your mother, now.'

But most of the faces in the crowd were not so kind. 'You saved other people,' someone laughed, 'so why can't you save yourself?'

Jesus knew why. It wasn't because his enemies had won. It was because God wanted him there—to take away all the bad things anyone had ever done.

Soon the sky grew dark and the earth shook. It was as if God's own heart was breaking. And then it happened.

'It's done,' Jesus whispered. And in the sadness and the dark, he died.

A Happy Day

It was very early. The birds were still in bed. And the sun had yet to open its bright eye on the world. The sky was grey and grainy. The air was cold. And three women walked slowly towards the graveyard.

Jesus was buried there. And the women were coming to visit his grave.

They talked in sad whispers. They cried. They held each other's hands. Jesus had been dead for three days, and they missed him very much.

Just as they reached the graveyard, however, some surprising things happened. The ground began to shake. The air began to tremble. And, quick as lightning, an angel flashed down from heaven and rolled the stone away from Jesus' tomb!

Everything went quiet. The ground stopped moving. But the women shook with fear.

'Don't be afraid,' the angel said. 'Come and see. The tomb is empty. Jesus is alive!'

Arm in arm, the women crept past the angel and into the tomb. The sheets were still there—the sheets they had wrapped round his dead body. But Jesus himself was gone!

'Where is he?' asked the women. 'What have you done with him?'

'I told you,' smiled the angel. 'He's not dead any more. He's come back to life. And he wants you to tell all his friends.'

The women looked at each other. They didn't know whether to laugh or cry. They could hardly believe it—that is until they hurried out of the tomb and ran straight into Jesus.

'Oh, Jesus!' they cried. 'It's true. You are alive!' And they fell at his feet, amazed!

'There's no need to be afraid any more,' he said. 'God has made everything all right. But I have a job for you. I want you to tell the rest of my friends that I am alive. Tell them I will meet them on the seashore, in Galilee, where all our adventures started.'

The women waved goodbye and hurried off to Jerusalem. The birds were singing now. The sun's bright eye was wide open. And they had the most amazing story to tell.

Other Bob Hartman titles
from Lion Publishing:

Old Testament Tales
from The Lion Storyteller Bible

The Lion Storyteller Bible

The Lion Storyteller Bedtime Book

Angels, Angels All Around

Cheer Up, Chicken!

Time to Go, Hippo!